Native American Library

CREEK
History and Culture

Helen Dwyer and Amy M. Stone

Consultant Robert J. Conley
Sequoyah Distinguished Professor at Western Carolina University

Gareth Stevens
Publishing

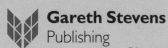

Please visit our website, www.garethstevens.com. For a free color catalog of all our high-quality books, call toll free 1-800-542-2595 or fax 1-877-542-2596.

Library of Congress Cataloging-in-Publication Data

Stone, Amy, 1947-
Creek history and culture / Amy M. Stone.
    p. cm. — (Native American library)
Includes index.
ISBN 978-1-4339-5964-6 (pbk.)
ISBN 978-1-4339-5965-3 (6-pack)
ISBN 978-1-4339-5962-2 (library binding)
1. Creek Indians—History—Juvenile literature. 2. Creek Indians—Social life and customs—Juvenile literature. I. Title.
E99.C9S836 2011
975.004'97385—dc22

                              2011004135

New edition published in 2012 by
Gareth Stevens Publishing
111 East 14th Street, Suite 349
New York, NY 10003

First edition published 2005 by Gareth Stevens Publishing

Copyright © 2012 Gareth Stevens Publishing

Produced by Discovery Books
Project editor: Helen Dwyer
Designer and page production: Sabine Beaupré
Photo researchers: Tom Humphrey and Helen Dwyer
Maps: Stefan Chabluk

Photo credits: Cover Marilyn Angel Wynn/Nativestock.com/Getty Images; AP/Wide World Photos: p. 36; Corbis: pp. 12, 19 (top), 34; Getty Images: p. 7 (Hulton Archive/Stringer); Native Stock: pp. 11, 14, 15, 17, 18, 19 (bottom), 20, 22, 23, 25, 26, 32, 33, 35, 38, 39; North Wind Picture Archives: p. 21; Peter Newark's American Pictures: pp. 16, 24; Phil Myers: p. 28; Shutterstock: pp. 29 (Steve Brigman), 30 (Larsek), 31 (Arthur van der Kooij).

Printed in the United States of America

CPSIA compliance information: Batch #CS11GS: For further information contact Gareth Stevens, New York, New York at 1-800-542-2595.

CONTENTS

Words that appear in the glossary are printed in **boldface** type the first time they appear in the text.

INTRODUCTION

THE MUSCOGEE IN NATIVE AMERICAN HISTORY

The Muscogee, or Creek, are a people originally from the southeastern region that is now Alabama and Georgia. They are just one of the many groups of Native Americans who live in North America. There are well over five hundred Native American tribes in the United States and more than six hundred in Canada. At least three million people in North America consider themselves to be Native Americans. But who are Native Americans, and how do the Muscogee fit into the history of North America's Native peoples?

Probable extent of dry land during the last ice age

CHUKCHI
SEA

SIBERIA

Bering Strait

ALASKA

CANADA

BERING SEA

Anchorage

Siberia (Asia) and Alaska (North America) are today separated by an area of ocean named the Bering Strait. During the last ice age, the green area on this map was at times dry land. The Asian ancestors of the Muscogee walked from one continent to the other.

THE FIRST IMMIGRANTS

Native Americans are people whose **ancestors** settled in North America thousands of years ago. These ancestors probably came from eastern parts of Asia. Their **migrations** probably occurred during cold periods called **ice ages**. At these times, sea levels were much lower than they are now. The area between northeastern Asia and Alaska was dry land, so it was possible to walk between the continents.

Scientists are not sure when these migrations took place, but it must have been more than twelve thousand years ago. Around that time, water levels rose and covered the land between Asia and the Americas.

4

The Cliff Palace at Mesa Verde, Colorado, is the most spectacular example of Native American culture that survives today. It consists of more than 150 rooms and pits built around A.D. 1200 from sandstone blocks.

By around ten thousand years ago, the climate had warmed and was similar to conditions today. The first peoples in North America moved around the continent in small groups, hunting wild animals and collecting a wide variety of plant foods. Gradually these groups spread out and lost contact with each other. They developed separate cultures and adopted lifestyles that suited their **environments.**

SETTLING DOWN

Although many tribes continued to gather food and hunt or fish, some Native Americans began to live in settlements and grow crops. Their homes ranged from underground pit houses and huts of mud and thatch to dwellings in cliffs. By 3500 B.C., a plentiful supply of fish in the Pacific Ocean and in rivers had enabled people to settle in large coastal villages from Alaska to Washington State. In the deserts of Arizona more than two thousand years later, farmers constructed hundreds of miles of **irrigation** canals to carry water to their crops.

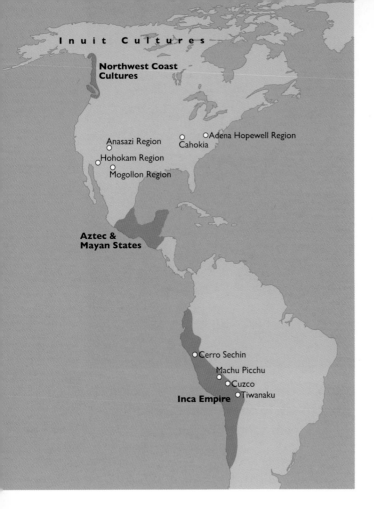

Inuit Cultures

Northwest Coast
Cultures

Anasazi Region
Hohokam Region
Mogollon Region

Cahokia
Adena Hopewell Region

Aztec &
Mayan States

Cerro Sechin
Machu Picchu
Cuzco
Tiwanaku
Inca Empire

This map highlights some of the main early Native American cultures.

In the Ohio River valley between 700 B.C. and A.D. 500, people of the Hopewell and Adena **cultures** built clusters of large burial mounds, such as the Serpent Mound in Ohio, which survives today. In the Mississippi **floodplains**, the Native peoples formed complex societies. They created mud and thatch temples on top of flat earth pyramids. Their largest town, Cahokia, in Illinois, contained more than one hundred mounds and may have been home to thirty thousand people. The ancestors of the Muscogee were part of this Mississippi culture. They developed tribal towns, each with its own chief and **council**.

CONTACT WITH EUROPEANS

Around A.D. 1500, European ships reached North America. The first explorers were the Spanish. Armed with guns and riding horses, they took over land and forced the Native Americans to work for them. The Spanish were followed by the British, Dutch, and French, who were looking for land to settle and for opportunities to trade.

When Native Americans met these Europeans they came into contact with diseases, such as smallpox and measles, that they had never experienced before. At least one half of all Native Americans, and possibly many more than that, were unable to overcome these diseases and died.

In the 1540s a Spanish army explored present-day Florida, Georgia, and Alabama. Many of the Native Americans of the region died fighting the Spanish or of diseases that the Spanish introduced. Faced with this threat, the Muscogee joined together with closely related peoples who spoke similar languages to form an **alliance** against Europeans. Despite this, many Muscogee were forced off their land during the eighteenth century.

Guns were also disastrous for Native Americans. At first, only the Europeans had guns, which enabled them to overcome native peoples in fights and battles. Eventually, Native American groups obtained guns and used them in conflicts with each other. Native American groups were also forced to take sides and fight in wars between the French and British. In 1813, after the creation of the United States, the Muscogee in eastern Alabama fought for the British against the Muscogee of western Georgia, who supported the United States. Up to three thousand Muscogee died fighting each other.

Horses, too, had a big influence in Native American lifestyles, especially on the Great Plains. Some groups became horse breeders and traders. People were able to travel greater distances and began to hunt buffalo on horseback. Soon horses became central to Plains trade and social life.

At the end of the 1700s, people of European descent began to migrate over the Appalachian Mountains, looking for new land to farm and exploit. By the middle of the nineteenth century, they had reached the west coast of North America. This expansion was disastrous for Native Americans.

A European illustration of Muscogee people from around 1800.

RESERVATION LIFE

Many peoples were pressured into moving onto **reservations** to the west. The biggest of these reservations later became the U.S. state of Oklahoma. Native Americans who tried to remain in their homelands were attacked and defeated. Most of the Muscogee moved to Oklahoma in the 1820s and 1830s.

New laws in the United States and Canada took away most of the control Native Americans had over their lives. They were expected to give up their cultures and adopt the ways and habits of white Americans. It became a crime to practice their traditional religions. Children were taken from their homes and placed in **boarding schools**, where they were forbidden to speak their native languages.

Despite this **persecution**, many Native Americans clung on to their cultures through the first half of the twentieth century. The Society of American Indians was founded in 1911, and its campaign for U.S. citizenship for Native Americans was successful in 1924. Other Native American organizations were formed to promote traditional cultures and to campaign politically for Native American rights.

Members of the Muscogee (Creek) Nation in Oklahoma about 1877. They include men of part European and African ancestry.

THE ROAD TO SELF-GOVERNMENT

Despite these campaigns, Native Americans on reservations endured poverty and very low standards of living. Many of them moved away to work and live in cities, where they hoped life would be better. In most cases, they found life just as difficult. They not only faced **discrimination** and **prejudice** but also could not compete successfully for jobs against more established ethnic groups.

In the 1970s, the American Indian Movement (AIM) organized large protests that attracted attention worldwide. They highlighted the problems of unemployment, discrimination, and poverty that Native Americans experienced in North America.

The AIM protests led to changes in policy. Some new laws protected the civil rights of Native Americans, while other laws allowed tribal governments to be formed. Today tribal governments have a wide range of powers. They operate large businesses and run their own schools and health care.

This map of North America highlights the main Native American cultural groups, along with the smaller groups, or tribes, featured in this series of books.

9

LAND AND ORIGINS

Chapter 1

THE CREEK OR MUSCOGEE NATION

About fifty-five thousand people count themselves as members of the Muscogee (Creek) **Nation**, the fourth-largest Native American nation in the United States. The term *Creek* comes from the name the Europeans gave to the group of Native Americans they found living along the streams and rivers in the Southeast in the late 1600s. Today, however, these Native Americans prefer the term their ancestors used — *Muscogee*.

Many Muscogee reside within the nation's eleven counties that make up the east-central part of Oklahoma. Others live and work across the entire United States.

Early ancestors of the Muscogee were part of the vast Mississippian culture, which arose about A.D. 800 and extended over much of the Southeast and middle of the continent. At its height, the Mississippian culture may have included 6.7 million people. The Muscogee first lived along the Ocmulgee River in present-day central Georgia and later spread to western Georgia and east-central Alabama.

Traditional Muscogee (Creek) homelands (shown in pink) stretched across the fertile countryside of today's Alabama, Georgia, and Florida and into South Carolina.

MUSCOGEE ORIGINS

The traditional story Muscogee tell of their origins explains that the Muscogee descended from the Cussitaw people.

10

Early ancestors of the Muscogee built large ceremonial mounds. This one, near Okmulgee, Georgia, reminds visitors that a thriving culture existed in North America long before Europeans arrived.

When the earth opened its mouth, out climbed the Cussitaws, who settled nearby. The earth shook and roared, then it ate some Cussitaw children, so the Cussitaws moved away, some toward the rising sun. On their way east, the Cussitaws followed a red river to its source, where they found a mountain with a great fire blazing on top. The Cussitaws helped themselves to some of this fire, and the Muscogee have kept it burning ever since.

The Muscogee Language

Muscogee refers not only to the people but also to their native language, which was originally called Muskogean. About four thousand people now speak Muscogee, most often during ceremonies.

Muscogee	Pronunciation	English
nokose	no-go-ze	bear
setempona-hokv	si-dim-bo-nah-ho-guh	telephone
vce	uh-je	corn
cokv espvlkv cuko	choh-guh is-bul-guh joe-go	library
cetto	jit-toh	snake
topv	do-buh	bed

Chapter 2

THE MUSCOGEE UNION

To the uneducated eyes of the Europeans who had come to North America in the late 1500s and 1600s, the Muscogee (Creeks) appeared to be a single people. Instead they were a union of tribes that included the Muscogee, Alabama, Coasati, Hitchiti, Mikasuki, Apalachee, Natchez, Yuchi, and Shawnee peoples. The Muscogee made up the most numerous and powerful tribe in the union.

From the late 1500s through the early 1800s, many Muscogee people lived along the beautiful Chattahoochee River that runs through present-day Atlanta, Georgia. Men and boys arose at dawn to catch some of the river's many fish.

Misnaming the Muscogee

Because the Muscogee lived near Ochese Creek, the British settlers in North America in the late 1600s called them *Ochese Creeks*, later shortening the term to *Creeks*. As the British met more Muscogee, they learned that they lived in two main areas — along the Coosa, Tallapoosa, and Alabama Rivers in present-day eastern Alabama and along the Chattahoochee, Ocmulgee, and Flint Rivers in present-day western Georgia. Nearly 100 miles (160 kilometers) of unsettled land lay between the two areas. The British called the Muscogee in eastern Alabama *Upper Creeks* and those in western Georgia *Lower Creeks*.

Union member tribes were called tribal towns. Each town had its own chief and council. Its members spoke a version, or dialect, of the Muscogee language. Although the dialects differed somewhat from one town or tribe to the next, members could understand one another.

As towns grew and the land could no longer support the population, some of the people left and formed new settlements. Over time, as settlements increased, and the larger Muscogee towns took over smaller, non-Muscogee tribal towns, the union grew into what became known as the Creek **Confederacy.**

TRADE BETWEEN THE MUSCOGEE AND THE EUROPEANS

By the 1700s, traders, explorers, and settlers from Great Britain, France, and Spain had all made their way to North America. Almost all the Europeans treated the Native Americans poorly if not brutally. Soldiers and settlers commonly burned Muscogee towns to create room for new settlements. The warriors of the Creek Confederacy, however, were often able to defend their towns against these European threats.

The Europeans mainly wanted deerskins, for which they would pay a high price, from the Muscogee. In exchange, the Europeans gave the Muscogee beads, guns, metal tools, European clothes, and copper and tin pots.

Britain, France, and Spain each wanted the Muscogee's goods for themselves. The leaders of the Upper and Lower Creeks feared that trading with only one country would lead to the other countries waging war against them. To decide what to do, the leaders formed a National Council, which agreed that trading with all three countries would offer the Muscogee the most protection against war.

Trading with all three countries, however, did not stop land loss. As more and more Europeans began settling in North America, they continued attempts to seize Muscogee land. The 1773 Treaty of August gave up, or ceded, a large portion of Muscogee land in present-day Georgia to Great Britain. These lands became the first British colony in Georgia. What little land the Muscogee kept fell within the boundaries of the new United States at the end of the American Revolution (the war between the American colonists and Great Britain) in 1783.

CREEK CIVIL WAR OF 1813–1814

In the early 1800s, the Shawnee Indian prophet Tecumseh urged Native Americans to rise up against white people. Whites would seize all Native American land and destroy Native American culture, he argued. The Upper Creeks agreed with Tecumseh. The Lower Creeks, however, believed that adopting white ways would lessen whites' hostility to natives and would ensure the Native Americans' survival.

More differences between the Upper and Lower Creeks surfaced. In the War of 1812 between Great Britain and the United States, the Upper Creeks sided with Great Britain, while the Lower Creeks sided with the United States. These differences led to the Creek **Civil War** in 1813. Under their chief, William McIntosh, the Lower Creeks defeated the Upper Creeks in the Battle of Horseshoe Bend, along the Tallapoosa River. By the time the Lower Creeks had won the war in 1814, between two thousand and three thousand Muscogee, most of them from the Upper region, had died. The power of the Creek Confederacy had been broken.

In its war against Great Britain in 1812, the United States had help from Lower Creek warriors. Upper Creeks supported Great Britain, a divide that contributed to the Creek Civil War a year later.

Lower Creek leader William McIntosh broke tribal law by signing a treaty without council permission. He was put to death for his crime.

MORE LAND LOSS

In 1824, the United States offered to buy all of the Muscogee's land in Georgia and two-thirds of their land in Alabama. Acting on their own, rather than on behalf of the National Council, Lower Creek leader William McIntosh and several tribal chiefs accepted the offer and signed the Treaty of Indian Springs. Signing a treaty without council approval broke Muscogee law, and the National Council persuaded the United States to cancel the treaty.

The council suspected, however, that it was only a matter of time before the United States would force all Native Americans to leave the Southeast. With council permission, Upper Creek leader Opothle Yahola signed the Treaty of Washington in 1826. Those who wanted to could stay in Alabama, but most Muscogee, including McIntosh's followers, moved west to Indian Territory in what is now Oklahoma.

THE TRAIL OF TEARS

The Indian Removal Act of 1832 called for Native Americans from the five largest tribes in the Southeast — the Muscogee, Choctaws, Cherokees, Chickasaws, and Seminoles — to **voluntarily** move to Indian Territory. Many Native Americans did move voluntarily, but those who did not were forced to go. Under orders from President Andrew Jackson, the U.S. Army marched nearly twenty thousand Muscogee to Indian Territory during the harshest part of the winter of 1836 to 1837.

REBUILDING LIVES

In Indian Territory, the Muscogee who survived their terrible journey met the small group of Muscogee who had moved there voluntarily ten years earlier. Still called Lower Creek, these were Muscogee who had adopted non-Indian customs such as owning slaves and holding land as **private property**. They

Except for babies, young children, and old people who rode in wagons, the Muscogee walked the 800-mile (1,300-km) trip to Indian Territory in today's Oklahoma. Unprotected from the severe weather and lacking food, nearly thirty-five hundred people died along the way.

lived along the Arkansas and Verdigris Rivers, where Coweta, Oklahoma, is today. The brother of William McIntosh, Roley McIntosh, headed their council.

While some of the newly arrived Muscogee joined this group, most settled 50 miles (80 km) away, along the Canadian River. Opothle Yahola headed their Upper Creek Council. Over time, differences between the two groups disappeared, and in 1839, they formed one National Council, led jointly by both sides.

THE CIVIL WAR DIVIDES THE NATION

During the 1860s, the Civil War between the northern Union states and the southern Confederate states nearly destroyed the Muscogee's new unity. In 1861, Daniel McIntosh, son of William McIntosh (and nephew of Roley McIntosh), supported the Confederate states. He formed a **regiment** whose sole purpose was to battle the mostly Upper Creek Muscogee who had remained loyal to the Union. To escape the conflict, the aging Opothle Yahola tried to lead nearly three thousand Muscogee, Seminole, and Shawnee people out of Indian Territory into Kansas. Three battles with McIntosh and his Confederate troops, as well as a terrible blizzard, killed almost all of the Upper Creeks, including Yahola. Because of the attacks on Yahola's group by the Confederate forces, many of the Upper Creeks joined the Union forces.

Even though the Upper Creeks had fought on the Union side, after the Civil War, the United States government forced the

Creek Nation as well as the Choctaws, Cherokees, Chickasaws, and Seminoles to give up all their lands in the western part of Indian Territory.

After the Civil War, rivalries among the Muscogee died down. In 1867, the Muscogee passed a new **constitution** that created a two-house legislature, a court system, and a principal chief. The tribal town of Okmulgee was chosen as the capital.

Highly respected Upper Creek Chief Opothle Yahola served the Muscogee well before and after the forced removal of Native Americans from the Southeast to Indian Territory. He encouraged the Muscogee to honor and maintain their traditional ways.

The Dawes Severalty Act

At the end of the 1800s, the Dawes Act forced the five southeastern tribes to divide jointly owned land into separate plots, or allotments. After allotment ended, in 1906, the U.S. government opened up what remained of former Indian Territory to white settlers.

By 1971, the U.S. courts had ruled that the Muscogee had a right to run their own government and elect their own officials. A principal chief was elected, and in 1987, the Muscogee drafted a new constitution.

U.S. government attempts to end the Muscogee Nation failed. Today, Muscogee leaders run services and businesses that help the people and culture thrive.

Boarding Schools and Bloomers

Before Oklahoma became a state in 1907, Muscogee children were educated at Muscogee Nation-owned boarding schools, and day schools were run by **missionaries**. The missionary teachers thought their pupils should learn "white ways." They washed out students' mouths with soap if they spoke their native languages and cut the girls' long braided hair to look more "American." After statehood, the state closed some Muscogee schools and ran others. By the 1920s, Muscogee students were attending state-owned public schools along with white students.

Boarding school children often found creative ways to break the many rules. Girls were made to wear bloomers, or long underwear, under their dresses, even in hot weather. When the girls left to take walks or attend dances in the boys' buildings, they hid the bloomers under large rocks.

Chapter 3

TRADITIONAL WAY OF LIFE

A LIFE OF ABUNDANCE

Before the Muscogees' (Creeks') first contact with Europeans in the mid-1500s and for two centuries more, **abundance** marked their lives. Muscogee lived near rivers and streams on fertile, easily farmed land that produced corn, beans, rice, sweet potatoes, and squash. By hunting deer, bear, turkey, wild birds, and rabbits, men provided ample food for their tribe. Women and children rounded out the Muscogee diet by gathering wild plants, nuts, berries, and roots. Button snakeroot, ginseng, and red cedar plants were used for medicines.

It may have been this abundance that shaped the Muscogee's thinking about ownership. Every tribal member enjoyed equal rights to the soil and what it produced, to the hunt and what it yielded, and even to household items. If one tribal member were to visit another member's house and say, "I need that knife," it would be freely given. All Indians were considered part of one family, and all men were called brother.

Muscogee women and older children used farming tools such as this one made of wood and shell. It helped loosen and ready the soil for sowing seeds.

Alexander McGillivray, a Creek chief in the late 1700s, tried to organize a group of southern Native American tribes to eject white settlers from Indian land.

POLITICAL AND SOCIAL STRUCTURE

Each town had its own chief who commanded respect and power. His council included a war chief as well as warriors and hunters. The chief held a council meeting every day, where tribal members could give their opinions. Councils decided where to house the food supply, when to hold ceremonies, and when to wage war. Every meeting started with drinking a ceremonial tea. While the Europeans described it as "the black drink" because of its color, the Muscogee called it "the white drink" because of its purpose — to make the mind and spirit pure, or white. During pleasant weather, the councils met outside in the public square. Cold-weather councils took place in the winter council house.

When geese flew south, traditional Muscogee men knew winter would soon arrive. To protect against harsh weather, they built homes out of tree limbs, bark, and plant fibers.

Religious ceremonies also took place in the town square as did stickball, a game much like modern-day lacrosse. Called "the little brother of war," stickball offered exercise and friendly competition. It was also used to settle land disputes between tribes and **clans**.

Family compounds surrounded the square and spread out for several miles along rivers and streams. Compounds included a house for storing food, as well as rectangular summer and winter homes, where people slept and cooked. House frames consisted of poles made from wood or woven plant fibers. The walls were made of mud and straw and the roofs built of tree bark. Animal hides **insulated** the winter houses. Each compound also included small family gardens managed by the women and girls.

A LIFE TOGETHER

Everyone within a tribal town shared responsibility for securing food. Women and children took care of the large **communal** garden. In the spring, they tilled the soil, making it soft and ready for planting. When the crops began to grow, the children — supervised by the tribal **elders** — chased away the deer and other animals that tried to eat the growing vegetables. Older boys and men did the hunting and fishing. Food belonged to the whole tribe, and no one ever went hungry.

Squash, corn, and beans grew in the Muscogee's communal gardens, which provided food for the entire village.

The Mother's Family Dominates

All children, both boys and girls, belonged to their mother's clan. Girls learned their roles from their mothers, while boys learned from their mother's brothers. Fathers, then, taught their sisters' sons (their nephews). Young men and women of the same clan were considered brother and sister, even if they lived in different towns and had never met each other. Clan members were not allowed to marry each other.

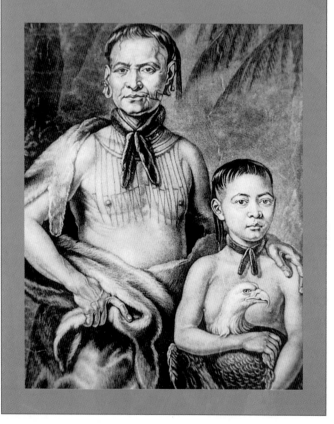

All Muscogee belonged to clans, such as the Bird, Bear, Turkey, and Wind clans, that determined ceremonial and other roles that families played. Clan ties added structure to the Muscogee society and created strong personal and political bonds. People of each clan lived in most towns. Since a person visiting a distant town would be housed and welcomed by his own clan members, the clan system linked the towns together.

NAMES AND ROLES

Until **puberty,** all Muscogee boys were called Chebon and all girls were called Hokte. At puberty, a clan name was bestowed. Sometimes the name was the same as a family member who had died.

Clan uncles acted as teachers and role models for their sisters' sons. Lower Creek tribal member Tomochicchi (on the left) may have taught his nephew, Toonahowi, important hunting and fishing skills.

Men and women fulfilled separate but equally valued roles. Men hunted and fished, waged war, and built shelters. Women planted and harvested crops; gathered roots, berries, and herbs; and made clothing, food, cookware, and decorative items. Before the Muscogee met the Europeans, women made everyday clothes and ceremonial sashes from deerskins and plant fibers. After European contact, the Muscogee traded deerskins for European goods, including cotton, wool, and beads, and then used them to make clothing. The women wanted to wear the same clothing as the early settlers coming into their homelands.

Muscogee women eagerly replaced somewhat rough animal skins with soft, colorful European cloth for sewing men's shirts and jackets as well as women's and girls' dresses and aprons. They often added bright beads, ribbons, and other decorations.

The Devil's Shoestring

The Muscogee sometimes used a plant called the devil's shoestring to catch fish. After pounding the plant's roots into a fine powder, the fishermen waded into the water and sprinkled the powder in it. The powder killed the fish, which would then float to the water's surface, where the fishermen would gather them up. The powder did not harm humans.

MUSCOGEE BELIEFS

Traditional Muscogee believed that the universe was made up of three worlds — "This World," "The Upper World," and "The Under World." Humans, plants, and animals lived in This World. Shaped like a large saucer, it floated on water. A bowl-shaped sky vault of solid rock covered it. The vault rose at dawn and dusk so the Sun and Moon could pass beneath.

The Upper World, above the sky vault, housed the Moon and Sun, as well as beings that looked like humans but were not subject to the same rules. Upper World beings could change shapes, for example. Just beneath the earth and water lay the Under World, home of ghosts and monsters.

The Muscogee lived in This World, trying to maintain a balance between the Upper and Under Worlds. They did this by keeping elements associated with the Upper and Under Worlds apart. Since fire came from the Sun in the Upper World and river or spring water arose from the Under World, it was the Muscogee's job to keep the two separate. A system of rules and **rituals** helped people remember how to maintain balance.

From corn, squash, and wild plants, the Muscogee women prepared a variety of healthful foods, shown here in a more modern setting. During the Green Corn Ceremony, or Busk, the Muscogee gave thanks for highly nutritious corn, which grew even when other crops failed.

The Muscogee honored the Sun, Moon, planets, and other beings of the Upper World but highly **revered** the Great Spirit, also called the Master of Breath. In frequent ceremonies and rituals, tribal members prayed for blessings that would yield successful hunts or abundant crops. The most important ceremony was the eight-day Green Corn Ceremony held in late summer, just after the corn crop had ripened. During the ceremony, the elders, the oldest people, put out the town fire that had been burning for the entire previous year and lit a new one. Embers from the new fire were used to light new family fires. Through dance and prayer, the Muscogee gave thanks for the harvest and asked and received forgiveness for any misdeeds.

ROLE OF MEDICINE MAKERS

Every town had medicine makers in charge of creating ceremonial and healing medicines from a variety of plants. Medicines cured illness, improved thinking, increased physical strength, and brought family and tribal peace. The main medicine maker, or the Heles-Hayv, was the most powerful among a town's medicine people. He chose new medicine makers, most often a child. The child needed to show an even temper and seriousness. It often took years to educate a new medicine maker.

A Born Medicine Maker

David Lewis, Jr., is a Muscogee medicine maker and member of the Bird clan who lives in Hickory Town, Oklahoma. He wrote a book called *Creek Indian Medicine Ways* so Muscogee people could understand their medicine tradition. Both his great-grandfather and his grandmother were medicine makers.

Lewis writes that before he was born, his father and grandmother made a medicine to see " . . . what kind of person I would be in fifty, sixty years. Would I keep our words **sacred**? . . . The minute I was born they gave me that medicine to see if I would take it. And they said, 'You drank that medicine like you were thirsty for water.' . . . And they were satisfied, they knew that I would keep it sacred."

Day or Night

The Muscogee have a **myth** to explain how day and night follow each other. They say that after the world was created all the animals argued about the length of day and night.

Eventually they held a meeting. Bear suggested that night was best and that there was no need for daytime. Then Ground Squirrel argued that daytime and nighttime should alternate, just like the dark and light rings on Raccoon's tail.

The other animals liked this idea and they voted in favor of it. Only Bear was still against it. He was so angry that he scratched Ground Squirrel's back with his claws. And so, all ground squirrels have had stripes on their backs ever since.

The Muscogee story mentions thirteen stripes on Ground Squirrel's back. Today, the thirteen-lined ground squirrel is a common species across much of the United States.

Like other species in the crow family, the blue jay is not a true songbird but it is able to mimic or "steal" bits of human speech and birdsong.

BLUE JAY'S VOICE

This story of Blue Jay is used to warn people to be cautious about what they say. The Muscogee people noticed that the blue jay stole eggs and food from other birds and that it mimicked the noises it heard. From these facts they created the following story.

A long time ago, Blue Jay had no song of her own, so she tried to steal one from other birds. She never succeeded, because all the birds guarded their songs very carefully. Then, one day, a crazy human who had drunk too much alcohol passed by, talking to himself all the time. As his words flew everywhere, Blue Jay saw her chance. She picked up all his words, out of the air and off the ground.

Later, Blue Jay tried out the stolen words, but the mixture of drunken words and the sound of the human voice only gave her a rasping, screeching noise. Since that time she has been unable to steal any better words and so she still makes a scratchy noise today.

Rabbit, Fox, and the Acorn Bread

The Muscogee have many stories of Rabbit and Fox trying to trick each other. In this story, Rabbit tricks Fox because Fox is too hungry to think properly.

One day on his travels, Fox saw Rabbit gazing at a pool of water. Fox had not had a meal for a very long time and he quickly decided that he would like to eat Rabbit. As Fox approached, Rabbit spoke to him. He told Fox that soon, as night fell, something special would happen. He knew that local Muscogee women had been making a huge circular piece of golden-yellow acorn bread, which they were just about to put in the pool as an offering to the creator god.

Fox was curious so, although he was hungry, he waited as the sun went down and darkness fell. To his surprise he saw what looked like a gigantic piece of acorn bread slide into the pool.

Fox was desperate to pull the bread out and eat it. Rabbit told Fox that if he drank the water in the pool, the acorn bread would be sucked

The rabbit of this story is probably the eastern cottontail, a species that inhabits the eastern half of the United States. It is not only foxes that like to eat cottontails. Other predators are hawks, eagles, owls, coyotes, and bobcats.

The fox is portrayed as a cunning animal in many other stories from around the world. The red fox is the most widespread species of the dog family in the world. Rabbits are part of its diet but it also hunts many other small mammals, birds, reptiles, and insects.

toward him. Fox thought this was a good idea. He began drinking, while Rabbit just watched and smiled.

At last, when Fox had drunk most of the water, he tried to bite the bread. At that moment, Rabbit threw a stone into the pool. Immediately, the golden disc broke up into ripples. Fox saw at once that the acorn bread was just the full moon's reflection in the water and he realized he had been fooled. He tried to chase Rabbit but he was so full of water that he was unable to move at all.

Rabbit moved some distance away and laughed at the success of his plan, while Fox moaned all night long. The Muscogee say that ever since then, Fox's relatives, the wolves and coyotes, have howled at the full moon out of sympathy for Fox.

MUSCOGEE LIFE TODAY

Chapter 4

THE MUSCOGEE NATION GROWS STRONGER

While the Muscogee (Creek) Nation has more members than ever before, it still faces many challenges. Jobs are scarce in many of the nation's counties. Due to years of little or no access to health care, many people, especially the older ones, suffer from serious health problems such as **diabetes** and high blood pressure.

To address these problems, the Muscogee (Creek) Nation provides a wide array of education, health, and employment

services. The nation owns and operates four health clinics and a hospital. The Office of Employment and Training helps people secure job training and jobs, and many Muscogee teenagers find work through the Summer Youth Employment program. They can acquire leadership skills by joining Youth Councils, where Muscogee history and language are also taught. The nation supplies more than twelve hundred **grants** and **scholarships** to Muscogee college students.

As this young man plays the ancient game of stickball, he affirms the long traditions of the Muscogee people.

The Muscogee (Creek) Nation owns and operates several cattle farms, three travel plazas, and four bingo halls, including this one in Okmulgee, Oklahoma. Profits help support educational and social services for the nation's members.

Forming the Muscogee National Business **Enterprise** has helped council leaders bring in money from the United States government. These funds support construction, business, and **manufacturing** projects that provide jobs and services for members of the tribe.

Ceremony, a Part of Life

Today, many Muscogee participate in Muscogee ceremonies as well as worship in Christian churches. The larger towns set aside special grounds, where people gather for ceremonial and stomp dances that feature dancing, singing, feasting, and storytelling. To maintain rhythm, women wear shakers made from turtle shells, while men use handheld turtle rattles. These rituals celebrate and honor the Great Spirit that continues to sustain the Muscogee people and their culture.

After learning how to sing and play the saxophone, poet Joy Harjo helped found the Poetic Justice Band. The band combines poetry with tribal, jazz, and rock music.

CREEK WRITERS

Born in Tulsa, Oklahoma, and a member of the Muscogee Nation, Joy Harjo studied painting and theater before later earning an advanced degree in creative writing. Her many writing awards include the Wordcraft Circle of Native Writers and Storytellers' Writer of the Year award for her 2001 children's book, *The Good Luck Cat*. In 2009, she published a coming-of-age poetic story called *For a Girl Becoming*.

Cynthia Leitich Smith, a member of the Muscogee Nation, loved writing stories while growing up in the 1970s. Unsure that she could earn a living as a writer, she became a lawyer but found herself writing stories during lunch. Finally, she traded practicing law for writing books. She has published several children's books, including *Jingle Dancer*, about a **contemporary** Muscogee girl in Oklahoma; *Rain is Not My Indian Name*, about a young photographer becoming active in Native American affairs; and *Indian Shoes*, a collection of short stories about a boy and his grandfather, set in **rural** Oklahoma and in Chicago.

Using imagination, patience, and skill, the Muscogee made traditional beaded bags such as this one. The Muscogee Nation offers classes in traditional arts like beading, basketweaving, and pottery making.

CREEK ARTISTS

Some Muscogee have merged their artistic talents with their interests in honoring and keeping Native customs alive. Muscogee artist Martha Noon-Tomah researches how early Muscogee made metal jewelry. She also teaches traditional jewelry-making techniques to young Muscogee. "If I reach one child it will be worth it," she says.

Dan Townsend is a well-known Muscogee shell carver. He creates medicine cups, pendants, and earrings. Some of his carvings are based on ancient designs and symbols from the southeastern United States, while others are original images of animals especially associated with water, such as dolphins, herons, and dragonflies.

After working with them a long time, you begin to understand that the symbols are really a written language, a medicine language, the breath of the creator.
Dan Townsend, shell carver

INDIAN ACTIVISM

Intent on destroying Native American communities, the U.S. government passed the Indian **Relocation** Act of 1953. Among other things, the act paid bus fares for Native Americans who agreed to move far away from their reservations or tribal towns. They also funded job-training programs in the new areas. Many Muscogee young adults left their tribal towns where jobs were scarce, hoping they could prosper in new locations. One such Muscogee was Millie Ketcheschawno.

In Oakland, California, and in San Francisco, Ketcheschawno formed friendships with many other young Native Americans. Throughout the late 1950s and early 1960s, they began reclaiming their traditions.

In 1963, the U.S. government shut down a federal prison on Alcatraz Island, just off the California coast in the San Francisco Bay. In 1969, the San Francisco United Council of Native Americans proposed that Alcatraz be turned into a **spiritual** and

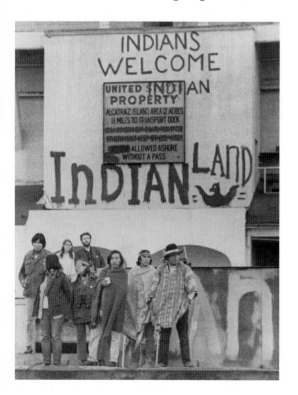

ecology center for Indians. When the U.S. government objected, the Native Americans, including Ketcheschawno, **occupied** Alcatraz Island. From 1969 to 1971, nearly fifteen thousand Native Americans visited or stayed in Alcatraz. Their actions showed that despite many attempts, the U.S. government could not break the many threads that bound Native Americans to a proud history and identity.

A group of Native Americans on Alcatraz Island stand under signs welcoming Indian occupiers to "United Indian Property" in 1969. With the occupation, Alcatraz became a symbol of growing Native American power.

THE POARCH CREEK BAND OF INDIANS

The Alcatraz occupation helped spark an **activism** that has touched Native Americans across the whole country, including the Poarch Creek Band of Indians. The Poarch Creek descended from the Muscogee who managed to stay in or near Poarch, Alabama, despite the forced removal of Native Americans to Indian Territory in the 1830s. Forbidden to speak their own language and to work for or be hired by white people, these Muscogee fought for and slowly won back many rights. The U.S. government recognized the Poarch Creek Band of Indians as an Indian tribe in 1984. Today, the band is made up of more than 2,300 members.

The Muscogee Nation of Florida

After abandoning their traditions, the Muscogee living in Florida resumed tribal traditions and their tribal council in the 1970s. In 2002, they applied for federal recognition, which could lead to funds for health care and housing and a name change — from the Florida Tribe of Eastern Creek Indians to Muscogee Nation of Florida. The Muscogee (Creek) Nation in Oklahoma, however, does not recognize the Florida group as an official tribe.

The government has recognized the Muscogee (Creek) Nation of Oklahoma and the Poarch Creek Band of Indians as official Muscogee tribes. The Florida Tribe of Eastern Creek Indians continues to work for recognition.

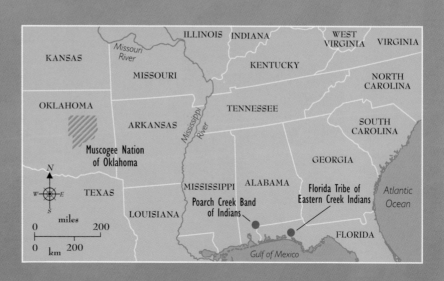

Chapter 5

A LIVING CULTURE

PROGRESS AND PRIDE

The leaders of the Muscogee (Creek) Nation work to ensure the well-being of all its members. Nation-sponsored social services reach many people, and new businesses and industries help make the nation's **economy** healthy and modern.

REMEMBERING THE PAST

In 2010, the Muscogee (Creek) Nation bought back its historic tribal **capitol** building, the Council House, from the city of Okmulgee and celebrated by holding a council meeting there. The Council House is a museum of Muscogee history and it hosts exhibitions of Muscogee arts and crafts.

A young Muscogee man stands ready to play the traditional game of stickball. This rough and energetic game is just one of several traditional Muscogee activities that have never died out. When they play stickball, today's Muscogees know they are preserving an important part of their heritage.

The Muscogee War Memorial in Okmulgee, Oklahoma, is located near the offices of the Muscogee (Creek) Nation. The war memorial honors veterans from several wars.

The Poarch Band of Creek Indians are trying to develop an interpretative center and memorial garden at Hickory Ground, near Wetumpka, Alabama. Hickory Ground is the site of an ancient Muscogee town. The interpretative center will educate visitors about the history of the site, while the memorial garden will house Muscogee human remains and funeral objects that are now scattered in museums across the United States.

Two Worlds

While they become more up-to-date and prosper, however, many people still keep their traditions. Children, adults, and elders join together in ceremonies to honor their ancestry and nourish their spirits. Muscogee elder and language instructor Pauline Pakosa Billy said that Muscogee live in two worlds. On the outside, they look and act like other Americans. Inside, however, their stories are very different. "All of us," she says, "remember what our ancestors endured." Despite countless invasions, betrayals, and efforts to destroy them, the Muscogee people remain strong.

TIMELINE

1500s–1600s	Survivors of the Mississippian culture migrate to the Southeast.
1540s	Hernando de Soto's Spanish army invades Muscogee territory and brings deadly new diseases.
1600s–1700s	Union of Muscogee tribes evolves into a multitown confederacy.
1680s onward	British, French, and Spanish establish settlements and trading posts next to Muscogee land.
1783	At the end of the American Revolution, the Treaty of Paris puts the Creek Confederacy into the newly created United States.
1790	Muscogee give up large areas of land in Georgia to the United States.
1813–14	Creek Civil War.
1814	Muscogee forced to give up land in Alabama to the United States.
1826	Muscogee are forced to give up all their remaining lands in Georgia to the United States.
1836–37	The U.S. Army removes more than twenty thousand Muscogee to Indian Territory in Oklahoma.
1839	The Lower and Upper Creeks in Indian Territory band together and form a Muscogee National Council.
1866	The Five Civilized Tribes sign a treaty with the U.S. government that causes them to lose the western half of today's Oklahoma.
1867	Muscogee living in Indian Territory pass a new constitution; Okmulgee is named the capital.

1890–1971	Even without federal recognition as a tribe, the Muscogee government continues to function, but the U.S. government must approve winners of the Muscogee government elections.
1892	Dawes Severalty Act begins to divide tribally owned land into individually owned pieces.
1896–1906	Indian Territory lands not divided by the Dawes Severalty Act are opened up for white settlement.
1936	Three Muscogee tribal towns in Oklahoma gain federal recognition.
1950	Creek Nation East of the Mississippi is established, based in Poarch, Alabama.
1970–80	Muscogee leaders create a new constitution, which the Muscogee people approve in 1979. Tribal name is changed to Muscogee (Creek) Nation.
1971	Due to government recognition, the Muscogee Nation gains the right to freely elect a new principal chief.
1980s	U.S. Supreme Court decisions affirm the Muscogee Nation's right to run its own courts and tax its people.
1984	Poarch Creek Band of Indians is recognized as a tribe by the United States.
2002	Muscogee Nation of Florida applies for federal recognition.
2003	Muscogee tribal citizens number over 55,000; about 71,000 people consider themselves full or part Muscogee.
2010	The Muscogee (Creek) Nation buys back its original capitol building from the city of Okmulgee.

GLOSSARY

abundance: a large amount; a quantity that is more than is needed.

activism: taking direct action to achieve a political goal.

alliance: a union formed for the benefit of the groups that are part of it.

ancestors: people from whom an individual or group is descended.

boarding schools: places where students must live at the school.

capitol: a building where a nation's laws are made.

civil war: a war between groups of members of the same nation.

clans: groups of related families.

communal: owned by a group of people rather than by individuals.

confederacy: a group of people, countries, or states united for a common purpose.

constitution: the basic laws and principles of a nation that outline the powers of the government and the rights of the people.

contemporary: happening in the present time.

council: a group of people chosen to meet regularly and manage a town or region.

culture: the arts, beliefs, and customs that form a people's way of life.

diabetes: disease in which there is too much sugar in the blood.

discrimination: unjust treatment usually because of a person's race or sex.

ecology: the study of living things and their relationship with each other and the places they inhabit.

economy: the way a country or people produces, divides up, and uses its goods and money.

elder: a tribal leader.

enterprise: business project.

environment: objects and conditions all around that affect living things and communities.

floodplain: the area of land beside a river or stream that is covered with water during a flood.

grant: a sum of money given by an organization for a specific purpose.

ice age: a period of time when the earth is very cold and lots of water in the oceans turns to ice.

insulated: prevented heat or cold from getting in.

irrigation: any system for watering the land to grow plants.

manufacturing: the making of things in large quantities using machinery.

migration: movement from one place to another.

missionaries: people who try to teach others their religion.

myth: a traditional story that explains beliefs or events in nature.

nation: people who have their own customs, laws, and land separate from other nations or peoples.

occupied: took control of land by settling on it.

persecution: treating someone or a certain group of people badly over a period of time.

predator: an animal that hunts and eats other animals.

prejudice: dislike or injustice that is not based on reason or experience.

private property: land or objects that belong only to one person.

puberty: the age when children begin to change into adults.

regiment: a military unit with a large number of soldiers.

relocation: the act of moving to a new place.

reservation: land set aside by the government for tribes to live on.

revered: regarded with deep respect.

rituals: systems of special ceremonies.

rural: relating to the countryside.

sacred: set apart for religious purposes.

scholarships: money for students to attend a school or college.

spiritual: affecting the human spirit or religion rather than physical things.

voluntarily: of one's own free choice; not being forced to do something.

MORE RESOURCES

WEBSITES:

http://www.bigorrin.org/creek_kids.htm
Online Creek Indian Fact Sheet For Kids in question-and-answer form with useful links.

http://www.indianlegend.com/creek/creek_index.htm
Enjoy some of the Muscogee legends, such as "How the Earth Was Made," that Muscogee people have told for hundreds of years.

http://www.native-languages.org/creek-legends.htm
This website has links to Muscogee stories online.

http://www.native-languages.org/muskogee.htm
This website includes guides to Muskogee alphabet, vocabulary, pronunciation, and grammar.

http://www.nativenashville.com/language/tutor_muskogee.htm
To learn some of the Muscogee language, visit this site, which covers everyday conversation as well as a few animals, foods, and numbers.

http://www.poarchcreekindians.org/xhtml/index.htm
The official website of the Poarch Band of Creek Indians.

http://themuscogeecreeknation.com/index.php?option=com_content&view=frontpage&Itemid=1
The official tribal website for the Muscogee (Creek) Nation.

BOOKS:

Boraas, Tracey. *The Creek: Farmers of the Southeast (American Indian Nations).* Capstone Press, 2000.

Gibson, Karen Bush. *Native American History for Kids: With 21 Activities.* Chicago Review Press, 2010.

Gray-Kanatiiosh, Barbara A. *The Creek (Native Americans).* Checkerboard Books, 2002.

Mueller, Pamela Bauer. *An Angry Drum Echoed: Mary Musgrove, Queen of the Creeks.* Pinata Publishing, 2007.

Murdoch, David S. *North American Indian (DK Eyewitness Books).* DK Children, 2005.

Rosinsky, Natalie M. *The Creek and Their History.* We the People, 2005.

Slusher-Haas, Kathy Jo. *The Southeast Indians: Daily Life in the 1500s (Native American Life).* Capstone Press, 2005.

Smith, Cynthia Leitich. *Indian Shoes.* HarperCollins Juvenile Books, 2002.

Smith, Cynthia Leitich. *Jingle Dancer.* HarperCollins, 2000.

Smith, Cynthia Leitich. *Rain Is Not My Indian Name.* HarperCollins, 2001.

Sonneborn, Liz. *The Creek (Native American Histories).* Lerner Publications, 2006.

THINGS TO THINK ABOUT AND DO

CELEBRATE

Plan a Native Americans' day that honors the Muscogee. Write stories that tell some of their history and choose traditional foods. Draw pictures of a Muscogee town from the 1700s.

UNDERSTAND

After reading the old people's "Story of Corn" at http://www.wm.edu/linguistics/creek/social/CornFable.pdf, see if you can figure out why the old woman told the young man not to climb the mountain and look around. In what ways did the young man help the townspeople? Why was corn so important to the Muscogee?

RUN FOR PRINCIPAL CHIEF OF THE MUSCOGEE NATION

If you wanted to win an election for principal chief of the Muscogee Nation, what promises would you make? Write a short speech telling voters how you would keep traditions alive and help people prosper.

WAR CORRESPONDENT

Pretend you are a newspaper reporter covering the Muscogee Civil War of 1813 to 1814. Write a short article that gives information about the war's causes and outcomes.

INDEX

hunting 5, 20, 23, 25

ice ages 4
Indian Relocation Act 36
Indian Removal Act 16
Indian Territory 16–17, 18, 19, 37

Jackson, Andrew 17

Ketcheschawno, Millie 36

language 8, 11,13
Lewis, David 27
Lower Creeks 13, 14, 15, 16, 17

McGillivray, Alexander 21
McIntosh, Daniel 18
McIntosh, Roley 17, 18
McIntosh, William 15, 16, 17, 18
medicine makers 27
medicines 20
migrations 4, 5
Mikasuki tribe 12
missionaries 19
Mississippi culture 6, 10
Muskogee (Creek) Nation 8, 10, 32, 33, 37, 38
Muskogee Nation of Florida 37
myths 10–11, 28–31

names 24
Natchez tribe 12
Noon-Tomah, Martha 35

Oklahoma 8, 10, 17
Okmulgee, Georgia 11

Okmulgee, Oklahoma 18, 33, 38
Opothle Yahola 16, 17, 18

Poarch Creek Band of Indians 37, 39
poverty 9

reservations 8, 9
rituals 26, 27

Seminole people 16, 18
Serpent Mound, Ohio 6
Shawnee tribe 12, 15, 18
Smith, Cynthia Leitich 34
society 21, 22, 23, 24, 25
Society of American Indians 8
stickball 22, 32, 38

Tecumseh 15
Townsend, Dan 35
trade 6, 7, 13, 14
Treaty of August 14
Treaty of Indian Springs 16
Treaty of Washington 16
tribal towns 6, 13, 23

Upper Creeks 13, 14, 15, 16, 17, 18

warfare 13, 18, 25
writers 34

Yuchi tribe 12